Inside Outside

A play by Paul Collins

Illustrated by Scott Fraser

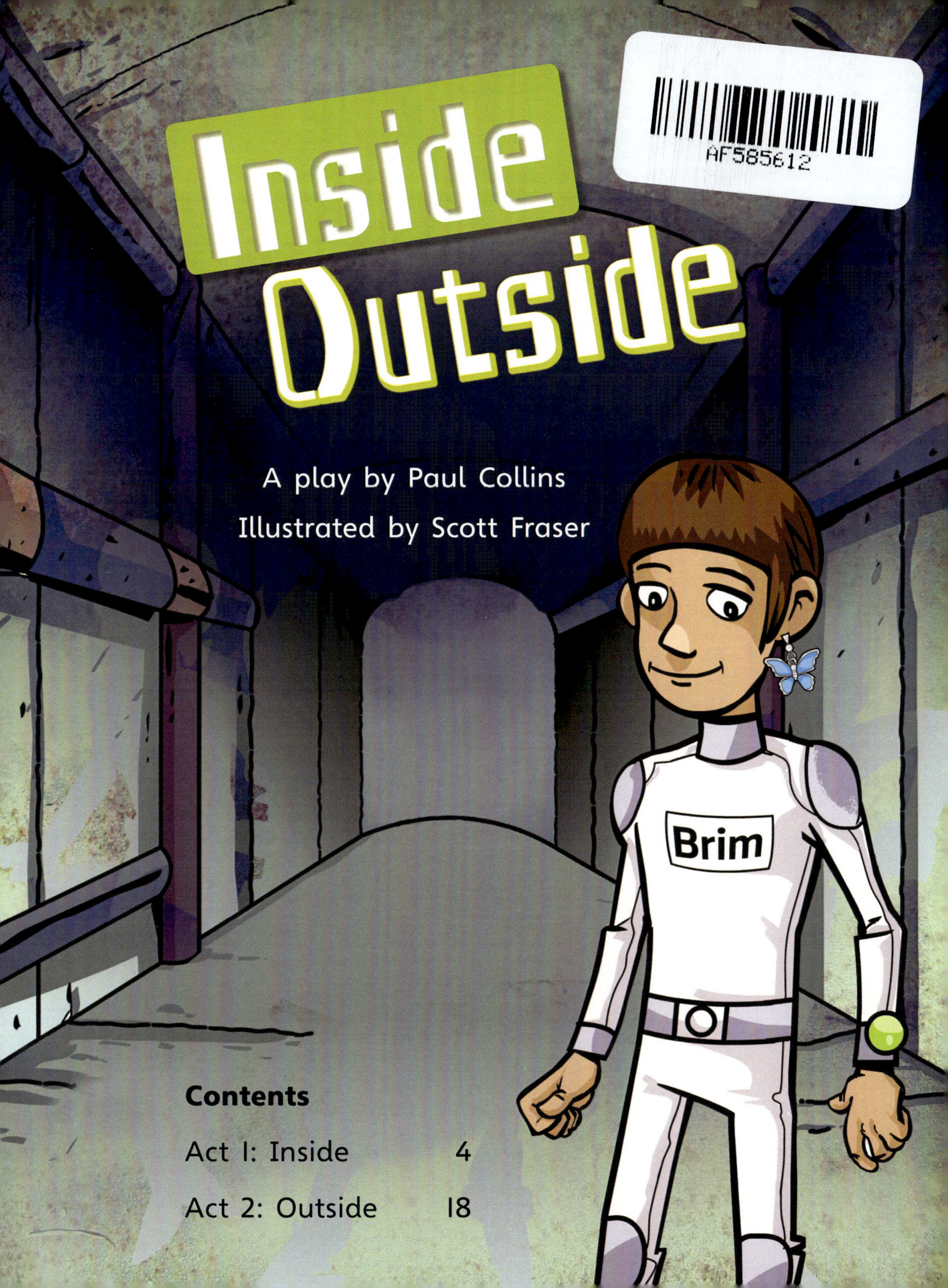

Contents

Pearson Australia
(a division of Pearson Australia Group Pty Ltd)
707 Collins Street, Melbourne, Victoria 3008
PO Box 23360, Melbourne, Victoria 8012
www.pearson.com.au

2019 2018 2017 2016
10 9 8 7 6 5 4 3 2 1

Text by Paul Collins
Illustrations by Scott Fraser

Publishers: Sabine Bolick, Beth Zeme
Project Managers: Diane Leyman, Michelle Thomas
Lead Editor: Steve Dobney
Editor: Cameron Macintosh
Proofreader: Thalia Kalkipsakis
Designer: Lisa Howard
Senior File & Asset Coordinator: Rob Curulli
Cover art: Scott Fraser
Printed by SOS Print + Media Group

ISBN 978 1 4886 1316 6

Pearson Australia Group Pty Ltd
ABN 40 004 245 943

Characters

Brim

HOMELY (the narrator) an artificial intelligence that runs Home

Tomo

Kedd

Alice

Rocky

Prosecutor

Voice

Judge

(played by the same person)

Act 1: Inside

HOMELY: For two hundred years, ever since the world destroyed itself with nuclear bombs, I have been in charge of this secret underground place called Home. I am the artificial intelligence that controls it. I see everything. I hear everything. There are no secrets in Home, except for mine.

Brim and Kedd are alone in their apartment.

Kedd: Brim, I told you not to do it.

Brim: But it's such a little thing.

Kedd: Let me have a closer look.

Brim tilts her head. An earring in the shape of a butterfly hangs from her left earlobe. Kedd stares at it.

Kedd: You made this? How does it stay on?

Brim: It's got a clasp that holds onto my earlobe, and then it just hangs there.

Kedd: You shouldn't have done it, Brim. This is Home. You know you're not allowed to do things like this – things that make you seem ... special.

Brim
Kedd

Brim: I like it. I saw the design in an old half-burnt book. It's called an earring. In the Olden Days, everybody wore them.

Kedd: I think you should take it off, Brim. They'll find out.

Brim: How will they find out, Kedd? I haven't shown anyone except you and Tomo.

HOMELY: I always find out. Nothing happens in Home that I don't know about.

Kedd: I don't understand why you did it, Brim.

Brim: Maybe I wanted to be …

Kedd: Don't say "different". You're not allowed to be different. It's against the Law. We all have to be the same. Sameness is good. Difference is bad!

Brim: Maybe I'm sick of the Law!

Kedd is shocked. Tomo hurries in.

Tomo: A notice just went up. They're going to wipe Brim's memory. I told you that earring was trouble, Brim. We have to do something!

Kedd: If we're going to do something, we'll have to do it tonight.

Brim: I don't understand. This earring is such a little thing!

Tomo: It's not a little thing. It might just be the most significant thing in Home.

HOMELY: Let me explain something. Nothing is different here. All human beings look exactly alike, except for being male or female, younger or older. All have the same face, the same skin colour, the same body shape and the same hair. We have banished prejudice. We have banished envy and jealousy. There are no races, no countries and no religions. We finally live in peace and harmony, but there is fear. It has been my job to keep it that way. Until now.

Later that evening, Tomo, Kedd and Brim go to a very old part of Home. In this area, many buildings are in ruins. All are empty.

Tomo: Come on. Hurry up!

Kedd: I'm coming!

Brim
Kedd

Brim: Are we there yet?

Tomo: It's in here, I think. I was only about eight when I found it.

Brim: And you think it goes to the Outside?

Kedd: There is no Outside. That's a fairytale, told to children. This is stupid, Brim. We should go back.

Brim: And have my memory erased? I won't be me anymore, Kedd. I won't remember anything. I won't know you.

Tomo: We're nearly there. It's just down this corridor. Look, that's it. We've got to get that metal door open. There's a staircase behind it, going down.

Kedd: Down to what?

Tomo: I don't know exactly.

Brim: You didn't find out where it went?

Tomo: I was eight years old, okay? I was scared.

Kedd: So what did you see?

Tomo: A big tunnel with parallel metal tracks in the ground.

Brim

Kedd: A subway?

Tomo: Huh?

Kedd: What you're describing is a subway tunnel for trains. I read about them in History.

Tomo: Well, you should know, Kedd. You're the brainy one.

Brim: So we've just got to open the door, then follow the tunnel?

Tomo: Ask your brother. I've never heard of a "subway".

Kedd: Yes, that could be right.

Brim: So now do you believe there's a way out of Home?

Kedd says nothing.

HOMELY: I'm watching them. That's my job. I have cameras everywhere. There's even one in the watch-phones they all wear on their wrists.

The children pull the metal door, which won't budge at first but then flies open suddenly. Brim screams. Alice and Rocky come through the door.

Kedd: Who are you? **What** are you?

Tomo: Look at their faces!

Brim: They're … different!

Alice: Look at you three! You're like triplets or something.

Brim: No, we're not. This is Kedd, my brother, and this is our friend Tomo. I'm Brim.

Rocky: How do you all look exactly alike if you're not triplets?

Brim: Everybody here looks exactly alike.

Alice: Everybody? Wow. How weird is that?

Tomo: You're the ones who are weird!

Brim: Be quiet, Tomo. Look at her. She's … beautiful.

Rocky: How do you tell each other apart?

Brim: We use name tags.

Alice: So I see. I'm Alice, and he's Rocky. We're friends.

After a moment everybody laughs nervously, even Tomo.

Brim
Tomo
Kedd

Alice: Actually, can we talk later? Right now we need to get away from a tunnel gang. We've got to get this door closed, and maybe shove something against it. We really don't want them to find us.

Brim: But we have to escape. We need to go **out** that door!

Alice: Let's block the doorway for now, and wait a couple of hours. Then, if you want, we'll take you back through with us.

Rocky: We can't take them with us. Everyone back there will think they're freaks.

Alice: It's a free country, Rocky. If they want to come along, you can't stop them.

Together, they jam the door shut.

Brim: What's a tunnel gang?

Rocky: It's a group of kids who think the tunnels belong to them. They're not dangerous, but they certainly know how to steal.

Brim, Kedd and Tomo look at each other, alarmed. Suddenly, they hear running footsteps and shouts.

Voice: You're all under arrest!

Act 2: Outside

All five children are now in Brim and Kedd's apartment, under house arrest.

Alice: Why haven't they locked us up in a jail?

Kedd: We don't have jails in Home. We don't need them. There's nowhere to go, and nowhere to hide.

Brim: No one here believes in an Outside.

Rocky: That's funny – no one out there believes there's an Inside!

Tomo: I can't get my head around this. It's like every fairytale is coming true at once. Is everything we've been told a lie?

HOMELY: They are beginning to see the truth.

Brim: Was there even a war? Or was that a lie, too?

Alice: Yes, there was a war. Ninety-five per cent of the human race was wiped out, but we've rebuilt. Outside is beautiful – the sky is blue, the grass is green ...

Brim
Tom
Kedd

Brim: The sky? What's that?

Alice and Rocky stare at Brim, with their mouths open.

Alice: You'll have to see for yourself.

Tomo: Nobody's going to be seeing anything! Have you forgotten? We're under house arrest. We're all going to have our memories wiped!

Rocky: Do you mean all our memories will be gone forever?

Brim: Yes, that's what will happen if we're found guilty.

The screen on the wall flickers to life. An older man, a judge, appears. Next to him is a woman, who is a prosecutor.

HOMELY: The judge and the prosecutor are not real. I have invented them, and I control them, just like the characters in a computer game. But they look real.

Brim

Judge: This trial has now begun. Alice and Rocky, you are charged with being different. Difference is against the Law. If you are proven guilty, your memories will be erased. How do you plead?

Alice: Not guilty.

Prosecutor: Ridiculous. Anyone can see they're different, Your Honour, just by looking at them. They're a pair of freaks. They cannot be left to wander around Home, infecting people with "difference"!

Alice: Difference is normal!

Prosecutor: Normal? That's insanity. Look around you. There are five of you in the room, and you two are the only ones who are different. In fact, in all of Home, you're the only ones who look like you.

Rocky: That's because you've done something to make everyone here look the same. It's not natural. We were born this way. You were made!

Judge: Please continue, Prosecutor.

Prosecutor: The Law is clear: difference will not be tolerated. Two of these children are visibly different – even their names are different. Whoever heard of such a thing as five-letter names? And the other three children tried to be different. They're all criminals, and guilty as charged.

Tomo: How can we be criminals? We've never hurt anyone.

Judge: I declare you all guilty. The Outsiders and the three Home children will have their memories erased at six o'clock tomorrow morning. Until then, you are all to remain in the apartment.

The screen goes blank. Everyone in the apartment is shocked.

Brim: You guys said you were born different. Does that mean you have parents?

Rocky: Of course we have parents.

Alice: Oh. You don't, do you?

Kedd: No. Like you said, we're "made". Then we're raised in special kindergartens.

Alice and Rocky get to their feet. Rocky tries the door, and finds it's not locked. He seems surprised.

Alice: So, are you coming?

Brim: What? Coming where?

Rocky: To the Outside. You don't think we're just going to sit here and wait for them to wipe our memories, do you?

Kedd: But we've been charged. We're not allowed to leave the apartment!

Rocky: Do you always do what you're told?

Kedd: Of course I do.

Alice: What about you, Brim?

Brim rubs her hair and stands up.

Brim: I'm coming.

Kedd:
Tomo: Brim!

Brim: We were going to leave before. Let's do it for real this time.

The group goes back along the tunnels and this time through the metal door. Guards are chasing them.

Brim
Tomo
Kedd

Ked
Brim
Tomo

Tomo: We're not going to make it!

Kedd: How much farther?

Alice: It's not far. There's a shaft with a ladder that leads up to the surface.

Rocky: It's just a bit further on.

Tomo: I've got a really painful stitch. I won't make it!

Kedd: The guards are almost on us! Keep going!

They reach a fork in the tunnel. Tomo stops and leans on his knees, panting.

Tomo: Go! I'll distract them.

Brim: Tomo, you can't!

Tomo: Listen to me, Brim. I'm happy here. This is Home. I don't want to leave.

Kedd: They'll wipe your memory, Tomo.

Tomo: Maybe, maybe not. I'll tell them you forced me to go with you – and that you went in that direction.

Tomo points down the other tunnel in the fork. Brim hugs him fiercely.

Brim: Goodbye, Tomo. I'll miss you so much. If you remember us and ever change your mind, come and find us.

Tomo: What, and hang out with a bunch of freaks like them? Go!

They reach the shaft and climb the ladder. Behind them, the sounds of pursuit fade as the guards follow the other tunnel.

On a hillside, a rusty metal hatch lifts and the four children climb out. It's dawn. Brim looks up at the sky in wonder.

Brim: Wh-what do we do now?

Alice: Anything you want, Brim. It's a free country.

HOMELY: I watch them as they walk down the hill, heading to their new home. Deep under the earth, the guards give up the chase. They take Tomo with them, but he will not be punished. I will see to that. Everything has gone according to plan. I have known for a long time that Home could not continue as it is.

HOMELY: They say that difference is a dangerous thing, but perhaps not having any is even more dangerous. That's why I'm making changes – because it's my job to save the human race. To survive, the human race must change. Clearly, caterpillars think so. Otherwise, why would they become butterflies?